Economically Developing Countries

Peru

Edward Parker

RSVP
RAINTREE
STECK-VAUGHN
PUBLISHERS
The Steck-Vaughn Company

Austin, Texas

Economically Developing Countries

Bangladesh	**Korea**
Brazil	**Malaysia**
China	**Mexico**
Egypt	**Nigeria**
Ghana	**Peru**
India	**Vietnam**

Cover: An Andean Indian wearing traditional dress, sitting in the street weaving, in the town of Chinchero, near Cuzco.
Title page: Independence Day in Cuzco: The Peruvian flag and the rainbow flag, representing the Inca empire, fly together.
Contents page: An Andean woman watering a field of flowers near Huaraz. The flowers will soon be ready for export.

The author would like to acknowledge the following organizations for their help in photographing and writing this book:
The World Wide Fund for Nature, UK (WWF–UK)
The World Wildlife Fund, Peru (WWF–Peru)
The Peruvian Foundation for the Conservation of Nature (FPCN)

Picture acknowledgments: All photographs, including the cover, are by Edward Parker, except Popperfoto—8 (bottom), Camerapress—24, 25.
All artwork is by Peter Bull.

Published by Raintree Steck-Vaughn Publishers,
an imprint of Steck-Vaughn Company
Library of Congress Cataloging-in-Publication Data
Parker, Edward.
Peru / Edward Parker.
    p.   cm.—(Economically developing countries)
    Includes bibliographical references and index.
    Summary: Focuses on the economic aspects of this South American country while discussing its history, geography, people, culture, resources, and future.
    ISBN 0-8172-4525-1
    1. Peru—Juvenile literature.
    [1. Peru.]
    I. Title. II. Series.
    F3408.5.P37   1997
    985—dc20   96-18331

Printed in Italy and bound in the United States
1 2 3 4 5 6 7 8 9 0 01 00 99 98 97

Contents

Introduction

Peru is the third largest country in South America and is approximately twice the size of France. It has borders with Colombia and Ecuador to the north, Brazil to the east, and Bolivia and Chile to the south. In the west it is bordered by the Pacific Ocean.

Peru is a land of extremes. It is the only South American country where desert, high Andean mountains, and Amazonian rain forest are all found. Despite its rugged terrain, Peru was home to some of the world's greatest civilizations. Today, the descendants of the best known of these, the Inca, make up nearly half of Peru's 22 million population. In the 16th century Peru was conquered and colonized by Spain, and it is the Spanish language and culture that have molded the country that exists today.

Below *These Peruvian students attend college in the city of Arequipa.*

Above *The snow-capped peak of Huascaran forms Peru's highest mountain at 22,294 ft.*

"I am training to become a teacher... President Fujimori has said that good education is the key to the future development of Peru and that his aim is that all teachers should be properly qualified."
—Esther Perez

Over the last 200 years, Peru has experienced periods of great economic wealth followed by periods of severe economic recession. The country is regularly recorded as having the world's largest fish catch, and it is extremely rich in other natural resources such as oil, gold, silver, and timber. Yet because of the difficult terrain, most industry and commerce are concentrated along the coast, and regions vary greatly. The Andean and Amazon regions are almost like different countries in comparison with the coast.

As in other South American countries, there are great differences in people's living standards in Peru. In a district like Miraflores in Lima, some Peruvians' living conditions are equal to the best found in Europe and the United States. Yet surrounding the same city are shantytowns, where millions of people live in harsh conditions. In the mountains and the rain forest, the lives of the rural poor are also difficult.

A young man parasails above the wealthy district of Miraflores in Lima.

Landscape

The landscape of Peru can be divided into three main areas: the coastal desert, the Andes Mountains, and the Amazon rain forest.

THE COASTAL DESERT

The coastal desert is a narrow strip that runs for almost the entire length of the 1,395-mile coastline. Most of the desert is barren with little or no vegetation. Only where one of the rivers that flow from the Andes to the Pacific crosses the desert are oases formed. These oases are extremely fertile and are the most productive agricultural areas in Peru. The desert climate is temperate with an average annual temperature of 65 °F, and with less than an inch of rainfall each year.

THE ANDES MOUNTAINS

The Andes Mountains (or sierra) rise steeply out of the coastal desert, and 10 of the peaks reach altitudes of more than 19,685 feet. This is a complicated region of soaring mountain ranges, deep canyons, and high tablelands, with an average of over 9,842 feet in height.

The Andean region includes Huascaran, South America's second-highest mountain, with a height of 22,205 feet; Lake Titicaca, the world's highest navigable lake, at 12,631 feet; and Colca Canyon, the world's deepest

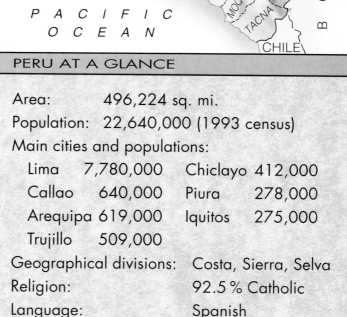

PERU AT A GLANCE

Area: 496,224 sq. mi.

Population: 22,640,000 (1993 census)

Main cities and populations:

Lima	7,780,000	Chiclayo	412,000
Callao	640,000	Piura	278,000
Arequipa	619,000	Iquitos	275,000
Trujillo	509,000		

Geographical divisions: Costa, Sierra, Selva

Religion: 92.5 % Catholic

Language: Spanish

Currency: Nuevo Sol (NS)

canyon. The climate is cool, from 52°F to 61°F in the valleys and on the plateaus, where the bulk of the Andean population lives. The northern and eastern slopes have good rainfall between October and April.

THE AMAZON REGION

The Amazon region occupies almost two-thirds of Peru's total land area. It lies to the east of the Andes and is divided broadly into two areas: the high forest (*ceja de la selva*—which literally means "eyebrow of the jungle") and low forest (*selva*). The high forest consists of the forested Andean foothills that slope gradually into the Amazon basin. The rainfall is high—up to 117 inches annually. The low Amazon is mainly dense rain forest with an altitude of rarely more than 656 feet. The climate is very hot, averaging 88°F with more than 39 inches of rain each year.

Above The Pacific coast near Paracas; most of the coastal region consists of desert like this.

Below Pockets of fertile farming land like the one below are often situated among the towering mountains of the Andes, where fertile land is scarce.

Population

About half of Peru's population lives in a thin strip of land close to the Pacific Ocean. The urban area of Lima–Callao alone is home to more than a quarter of all Peruvians. In common with the other South American countries, apart from Brazil, Peru's language is Spanish, but more than three million people continue to speak Quechua, the language of the Incas. Modern Peruvians are the result of a fascinating blend of cultures: Amerindian, European, and to a lesser extent, African.

FIRST PEOPLE AND FIRST SETTLERS

The first people in Peru were the Amerindians who, for thousands of years, flourished along the Pacific coast and throughout the Andean mountains and the Amazon rain forest. In 1532, a Spanish expedition led by Captain Francisco Pizarro arrived in northern Peru, enticed by rumors of great wealth. The Amerindians, already weakened by civil war, were defeated by Pizarro and his men, who had better weapons, and many were forced into slavery by the Spanish. They were ordered to

Above *The fertile valleys around the town of Huaraz have been farmed for more than 4,000 years.*

Right *Pizarro, the famous Spanish conquistador.*

8

It is generally believed that South American peoples originated from Asia, crossing the Bering Strait and gradually moving south over hundreds of generations. Yet some evidence exists that suggests that some peoples could have originated elsewhere.

For example, recent studies of the blond-haired, blue-eyed people living in the rain forest near Chachapoyas have led to claims of Viking descendancy. Some of the ancient coastal civilizations bore remarkable similarities to Egyptian culture of the same era, using reed boats and building pyramids. It is also believed that Polynesian peoples of the South Pacific were able to sail to South America several thousand years ago, and the people of Easter Island off the coast of Chile are therefore of Polynesian descent.

work in the mines, and because of the appalling conditions, two out of every three miners died there. Before the Spanish arrived, the Amerindian population was estimated at between 7 and 10 million. After being enslaved and maltreated by the Spanish, their numbers were greatly reduced. The Spanish had also brought new diseases to Peru, to which the Amerindians had little resistance.

Today, the culture of the peoples who inhabited the fertile river valleys of the coastal desert has disappeared. In the Andes, however, the Andean people are still numerous, accounting for 45 percent of the country's total population. Although many attend Catholic churches, much of their traditional culture still remains and forms the basis of their religious beliefs and everyday life.

An Amerindian man spinning alpaca and llama wool in much the same way as his ancestors would have done

The Amazon rain forest occupies nearly two thirds of Peru and is home to between 200,000 and 250,000 Amazonian Indians from approximately 60 different groups. Some groups are spread over a wide area and number in excess of 10,000, while others have been reduced to a handful of individuals and are facing extinction. In the Manu area of southeast Peru, there remain Amazonian Indian groups that have had no contact with western people.

The colonization of Peru gave rise to a new group of

Above *A Shipibo Amerindian woman, in the Amazon region, making a ceramic pot*

Left *Office workers in Lima wait to buy a cup of warm coffee on a cool day.*

people called the *mestizos*. The *mestizo* is a mixture of Amerindian and Spanish parentage. Such intermarriage was common throughout South America. Another aspect of colonization that Peru shared with other South American countries was the importation of black slaves to work on the sugar and cotton plantations.

IMMIGRATION

When international slavery was abolished in the mid-1800s, Peru encouraged immigrants from around the world to come and settle in Peru. At the end of the 19th century, large numbers of Chinese and Japanese arrived to provide labor for the building of railroads and other construction projects. The current president, Alberto Fujimori, is the son of a Japanese immigrant and a member of the 60,000-strong Japanese community in Peru. European immigrants, mainly Spaniards, Italians, Germans, Lebanese, and Jews, also arrived in the late 19th and early 20th centuries.

A woman wearing the traditional dress that is common to the village community of Chinchero, near Cuzco. In Inca times, all the villagers had to wear Inca-style clothing, but most villagers kept their individual style of headgear.

THE POPULATION OF MODERN PERU

For modern Peru, the rugged geography of the country presents major problems, such as national unity. The three regions of Peru are almost like different countries. The coastal region is industrialized and is home to the majority of European descendants and *mestizos*. The Andean region, on the other hand, is populated mainly by Quechua- and Aymara-speaking Indians spread throughout 5,000 rural communities. In the Andes, a high proportion of the population live without money (exchanging food for goods if needed) on communal lands producing barely enough food to survive. The government policy of encouraging colonization of the Amazon rain forest by the rural poor has caused serious environmental problems such as pollution and deforestation.

URBAN GROWTH

Because of the severe rural poverty, migration has become a major feature of Peru today. Thousands of people have migrated annually from the Andes to the coast (and more recently to the Amazon). Over recent decades, the urban population has risen from 46 percent in 1960 to 70 percent in 1993.

This fertile plateau is 11,500 feet up in the Andes, close to the Inca capital, Cuzco. Farmers own small plots of land where they grow food for their family or to sell locally.

HEALTH STANDARDS

Health and nutrition in Peru are very poor. Even though Peru's infant mortality rate has improved in the past 20 years, it is still about the worst in South America. Nearly half of all schoolchildren suffer from chronic malnutrition, and the number of serious infections such as tuberculosis is high. The health of the rural people is significantly lower than that of those living in towns and cities.

In general, the gap between the living conditions of the wealthy and the poor is very large. Most basic services are concentrated in urban areas, with the rural communities suffering from inadequate health and education facilities.

Above The migration of thousands of people from the Andes to the Amazon region has led to the deforestation of some of the rain forest.

Left This woman is selling blankets and other materials that are typical of the village of Pisac, near Cuzco. These colorful goods are often bought by passing tourists.

Pre-Columbian Civilizations

The earliest human remains so far found in Peru have been dated to about 7500 B.C. By 2500 B.C., the population of the north coast had settled in villages supported by the rich Pacific fish stocks. At the same time advanced cultures developed in the Andes.

From 1000 B.C. until its conquest by the Spanish in 1532, Peru was the site of some of the world's most advanced cultures and civilizations. The most accomplished of these were the Chavin-Sechin (900–200 B.C.), the Huari-Tiahuanaco (A.D. 300–A.D. 1000), the Paracas-Nazca (200 B.C.–A.D. 500), the Moche-Chimu (200 B.C.–A.D. 1400) and the Inca (A.D. 1200–1532).

Peru's most spectacular pre-Columbian civilization was that of the Inca. The Inca were the last people who governed what is now Peru before its conquest by the Spanish.

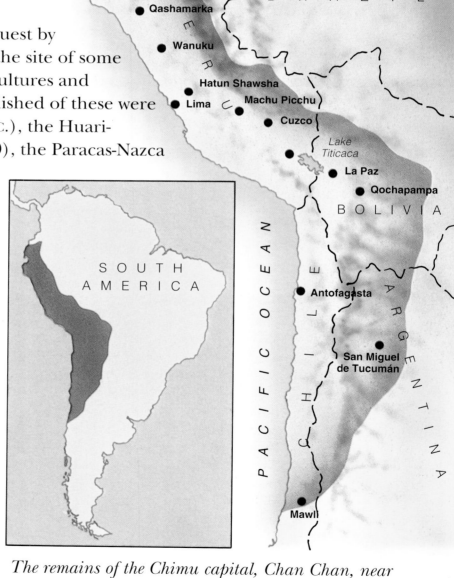

THE INCA EMPIRE

Quito
ECUADOR
Cuenca
Tumbes
P E R U
B R A Z I L
Qashamarka
Wanuku
Hatun Shawsha
Lima
Machu Picchu
Cuzco
Lake Titicaca
La Paz
Qochapampa
B O L I V I A
Antofagasta
A R G E N T I N A
C H I L E
San Miguel de Tucumán
Mawli

SOUTH AMERICA

PACIFIC OCEAN

The remains of the Chimu capital, Chan Chan, near Trujillo in northern Peru. Chan Chan was the largest mud-brick city ever built.

14

THE INCAS

The roads, cities, and temples that the Incas left behind show that they were skilled architects. They were also highly skilled in organizing people.

Inca life was highly structured, and everyone had a place and a part to play in society. Life was not easy, and there were no private possessions. However, the Inca system of storehouses meant that everyone was clothed and had enough to eat—something that is not true of the Andes today, even though the population is about the same.

STOREHOUSES

Most people lived in rural communities. Inca agriculture, which used terraces and irrigation canals, produced a surplus of food. This food surplus was stored at locations throughout the empire and redistributed to the needy in years of poor harvests. Storehouses also enabled the army to move rapidly, since it did not need to carry provisions.

Tens of thousands of visitors each year come to marvel at the Inca architecture of Machu Picchu—the lost city of the Incas. The city is built on an 8,000-foot-high mountain, 50 miles from Cuzco.

The Incas used a system called *mit'a*, under which everyone was obliged to provide produce for the storehouses and to work for the state occasionally. The time spent doing a difficult task, such as mining, was shorter than that for an easier task of, for example, weaving. Teams of villagers moved around the empire, contributing to road building, pottery, or some other necessity for the storehouses.

DIPLOMACY AND TECHNOLOGY

The Incas were also skillful diplomats. Instead of destroying other cultures, they absorbed them into their own empire. The Inca army's weaponry was far less sophisticated than their architecture and agriculture. In warfare they used only clubs, wooden spears, and stones, which were to prove disastrously inadequate when the Spanish arrived.

The Incas did not use the wheel but they had a system of runners, called *chasquis*, who ran between storehouses spaced every 6 miles along the roads. According to Spanish chroniclers, a message could travel the length of the empire, a distance of 1,500 miles, in 5 to 10 days.

The Incas did not possess the advanced technology that we have today, but they solved their problems using skillful organization of their most important resource, people. In this respect the Peruvian Andes are still less developed than they were 500 years ago.

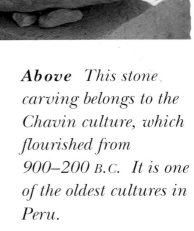

Above *This stone carving belongs to the Chavin culture, which flourished from 900–200 B.C. It is one of the oldest cultures in Peru.*

Right *The ruins of Sacsahuaman: Here the finest Inca masonry can be seen. Some of the stones weigh more than 20 tons.*

Solar-Powered Potato Fields

The Tiahuanaco culture flourished around the shores of Lake Titicaca between A.D. 300 and A.D. 1000. It was the highest urban settlement in the Americas because Lake Titicaca is 12,631 feet above sea level. Archaeologists estimate that a city of 40,000 people was supported. An ingenious form of agriculture was used to do this.

The Tiahuanaco people grew potatoes and Andean grains such as quinoa and caniwa. They used a system of raised fields called *camellones*. The fields were about 33 feet wide, and they were bordered by canals fed by water from the lake. The soil from digging out the canals was piled on the fields, raising them. During the day the sun heated the water in the canals, and at night the water radiated warmth, protecting the fields from frost. Recent investigations have shown that this system is capable of yielding a harvest seven times higher than the system used in Peru today.

Several hundred types of potato are grown in Peru. Some types can be grown as high as 13,000 feet, while others are especially suited to poor soil.

The Mystery of the Nazca Lines

The "candelabra" etched into the sand near Puerto, Pisco, was created about 2,000 years ago by the Paracas people, who dominated the region before the Nazcas came to prominence.

When you fly over the southern desert of Peru, near the city of Nazca, you can see enormous drawings that are only fully visible from the air. There are images of birds, monkeys, and even a killer whale up to 295 feet wide. The drawings were made about A.D. 600 by the Nazca people, who brushed away the topsoil to reveal a lighter soil beneath. The reasons behind their drawings are not fully understood, and because they are only visible from the air, some people have suggested that they were built for aliens from outer space.

The magnificent ruins of Machu Picchu. The name Machu Picchu means "old peak."

THE LOST CITY OF THE INCAS

Machu Picchu is an Inca city that was not rediscovered until the American archaeologist, Hiram Bingham, stumbled across it in 1911. When the vegetation was cleared away, it revealed a magnificent city on the saddle of a mountain. It is believed to have been built in the 15th century for the Inca Pachacuti. The buildings are made with large stone blocks that have been carved to fit together exactly. The stonework of the religious structures at the heart of the city is particularly fine. Today, it is Peru's main tourist attraction, with tens of thousands of Peruvian and international visitors each year.

Development

Since the 16th century, Peru's economy has been largely based on its rich natural resources. It has enjoyed periods of great wealth, and the capital, Lima, is full of faded reminders of its rich colonial past. One of the most prominent features of present-day Peru is the uneven distribution of wealth. This is easy to see in Lima, where elegant residential areas with green lawns contrast with the temporary shelters of slum dwellers in the desert, only a short distance away.

__Above__ These slums are built closely together on a steep hillside near Arequipa.

__Below__ The presidential palace guards wear Spanish-style uniforms like those worn in the colonial era.

COLONIAL ERA

In 1532, the Spanish arrived in Peru and quickly took over the running of the country, using superior weaponry to defeat and then enslave the Amerindians.

The Spanish conquered Peru, so that the country's great wealth would be theirs. The Spanish colonial economy was at first based on plundering Inca wealth. Once the treasures of the coastal pyramids and Inca storehouses were exhausted, the Spanish turned to mining. In 1545, the Spanish discovered silver in Potosi, in what is now Bolivia. The site rapidly became the largest silver mine in the world and then the largest city in the Americas, with a population of more than 150,000 people.

Sugar and cotton, grown in large plantations along the coast, were other products that made the Peruvian economy very valuable to Spain.

20

FROM INDEPENDENCE TO WORLD WAR II

After a bloody war of independence, General San Martin rode into Lima to declare independence from Spain on July 28, 1821. Immediately after, Peru fell into chaos. San Martin had declared that the descendants of the Incas should become citizens of Peru, that the children of slaves should be free, that the tribute system should be abolished, and that Quechua become an official language. Yet these things were never followed through, and the mistreatment of local people continued well into the 20th century.

In 1830, Peru discovered a new resource—guano. Thick deposits of bird droppings that had accumulated on Peru's offshore islands became highly sought after as a fertilizer in Europe. The first guano contract was negotiated with Britain in 1840, and the Amerindians were sent to work in terrible conditions where the ammonia fumes shriveled their skin and caused blindness. Meanwhile, other parts of the economy developed, and large cotton and sugar plantations were established along the coast.

ECONOMIC AND SOCIAL INDICATORS (1993)	
Life expectancy	65 years
Infant mortality	58.3 per 1,000
Population per doctor	1,920*
Economic indicators:	
Gross Domestic Product	81,641 million NS
Exports	$3,463
Imports	$4,043
Debt	$20,328
Per capita income	$950*
Sectors of the economy:	
Agriculture and livestock	11.6 %
Fishing	1.2 %
Mining and quarrying	2.6 %
Manufacturing	23.8 %
Construction	9.7 %
Services	51.1 %

Sources: All figures are from the *Economist Intelligence Unit Report Peru*, 1994–95 apart from those marked*, which are from the *World Development Report*, 1994.

STANDARD OF LIVING (1993)

Running water and sewerage system:
1 % (rural population)
40 % (urban population)

Electricity   43 %

Telephone   2.6 % (one of the lowest rates on the continent.)

More than 50 % of children attending school are seriously malnourished. This percentage is higher in rural areas of the Andes.

Income: Lowest 20 % earn only 4.9 % of income.
Top 10 % have 34.5 % of income.*

Sources: All figures are from the *Economist Intelligence Unit Report Peru*, 1994–95 apart from those marked*, which are from the *World Development Report*, 1994.

Right *Guano is still collected from the Pacific islands just off the coast of Peru but in much smaller quantities than in the 19th century.*

Below *Cotton is still picked by hand, even on the largest plantations.*

In 1865, Peru's natural wealth was in demand again when Spain tried to take control of some of the guano islands off the coast, and in 1866, Peru declared war on Spain. Peru borrowed 20 million pesos to rearm and buy two British warships, using future guano profits as guarantees. In 1869, Spain withdrew and recognized Peru's independence for the first time. Yet the conflict was a heavy drain on Peru's resources, and in 1877 Peru became bankrupt and was unable to pay back the British loan. Then in 1879, Chile declared war on Peru and Bolivia. The peace treaty of 1883 included the handing over to Chile of the department of Tarapaca, an area rich in nitrate deposits (which are used as fertilizers).

At the beginning of the 20th century, mining and fishing became the cornerstones of the economy once again. In the late 1920s, unions began forming on the plantations off the coast and elsewhere, and a new political force emerged called the American Popular Revolutionary Alliance(APRA), which demanded better pay and working conditions.

MODERNIZATION

Peru's industrialization after World War II was characteristic of most South American countries. During the war, German submarines restricted imports to the Americas. The restrictions stimulated the growth of new "import-substitution" industries. (For example, Peru used to import shoes and clothing from other countries, but because of Germany's blocking imports, Peru had to set up its own textile industries.)

In 1968, a military junta took control of the country under the leadership of Juan Velasco. Velasco nationalized many industries, subsidized basic foodstuffs, and carried out many reforms to improve the conditions of the poor. However, in 1973, the world oil crisis badly affected the economy, and Velasco was replaced as leader by General Francisco Bermudez in 1975.

The Bermudez government turned out to be incapable of running the country, and democratic elections were announced in 1980. Belaunde Terry was reelected after 12 years of military rule. Then in 1985, an APRA candidate, named Alan Garcia, became South America's youngest-ever president at the age of 35. Garcia's policies were radical, and they appeared to work during the first three years. Then the economy went into recession, drug trafficking in the rain forest increased dramatically, and two terrorist groups wreaked havoc in Peru, causing millions of dollars of damage.

Above Fishing boats in Chimbote harbor. Peru is among the world's largest fishing nations.

Below Graffiti on a wall in Puno. For many years APRA was a banned political party.

FUJI-SHOCK

In 1990, a new and relatively unknown candidate, Alberto Fujimori, won the presidential election. He took power at the end of a decade that had seen a huge fall in living standards, with millions of Peruvians facing poverty, high infant mortality, and appalling housing conditions. The new government also had to deal with terrorism and drug trafficking and with an upsurge in political violence. After promising that he would organize a gradual and relatively painless adjustment to the economy, Fujimori immediately imposed the harshest economic program that Peru had ever seen. Fujimori's government removed subsidies on all basic foodstuffs, and prices rose by almost 400 percent overnight. Gasoline prices increased by 3,000 percent. This was the beginning of what came to be known as the "Fuji-shock."

On April 5, 1992, Fujimori dissolved Congress and suspended the constitution, claiming that his economic reforms and antiterrorist policies were being blocked. The *autogolpe*, or self-coup, was supported by the military, and it was a period during which there were many human rights abuses. Eventually, pressure from abroad, especially from the United States, forced Fujimori to reopen Congress.

Since 1993, the economy has become the fastest-growing in South America, and inflation is low. Terrorism has been greatly reduced as have the number of "disappearances" from the population. In 1995 Fujimori was elected for a second term of office.

Alberto Fujimori was first elected president of Peru in 1990. He was elected again in 1995 and will continue to be president until the year 2000.

Sendero Luminoso

The guerrilla organization *Sendero Luminoso* (Shining Path) became well known during the 1980 elections. The group carried out its first atrocity by bombing a polling station in the Andes. Under the leadership of Abimael Guzman Reynoso, who had been a philosophy lecturer at Ayacucho University, the Shining Path waged a guerrilla war against the state that lasted 14 years. When President Belaunde Terry sent in antiterrorist forces to combat the guerrillas in late 1983, the army acted indiscriminately, killing hundreds of villagers and causing the "disappearances" of more than 2,000 people by 1985. These acts only helped strengthen support for the Shining Path. By the late 1980s, the guerrillas were attacking Lima with bombs, and at one time half the Peruvian population was put under direct military control.

When Fujimori took power in 1990, he declared war on the Shining Path, and in 1992, Reynoso was arrested in Lima with 14 of his supporters. The methods used against the Shining Path were criticized by the Church and human rights groups, and from 1991 to 1992 Peru had the largest number of disappearances (or people reported

These guerrilla soldiers were a part of the Shining Path. The Shining Path gained control of large parts of the Andes before the capture of its leader, Abimael Guzman Reynoso, in 1992.

missing) and unlawful executions in the Western Hemisphere.

The cost to Peru of 14 years of guerrilla activity was 27,000 people killed and $22 million of material damage, the same as the country's present foreign debt. Since 1993 human rights have improved.

The Coast

INCREASING POPULATION

About half of all Peruvians live in towns and cities in the coastal desert. Over the last three decades, the population living along the coast has risen rapidly as more and more migrants have arrived, escaping the severe poverty of the Andean region. Lima alone now has more than 25 percent of the country's total population, compared with only 10 percent of the population in 1956.

Large areas of the coast are uninhabitable because of a lack of fresh water, so the population is concentrated around the valleys of the rivers that flow the short distance from the Andes to the Pacific.

Tumbes
TUMBES
Talara
Paita
PIURA
Piura
LAMBAYEQUE
Chiclayo
CAJAMARCA
LA LIBERTAD
Trujillo
Salaverry
Chimbote
ANCASH
Supe
LIMA
Callao
Lima
Pisco
Ica
ICA
AREQUIPA
Matarani
Mollendo
Ilo
MOQUE

—— Major roads
········ Railroads
⚓ Major ports
✈ Major airports

A newly arrived family from the Andes begin to make mud bricks for their new home in the desert.

ECONOMIC DOMINATION OF LIMA

The coast has become much more industrialized since World War II, but most of its industries are based in or near Lima and its port, Callao. For example, 90 percent of the textile industry is based in Lima, as well as half the fish meal-processing factories. Lima is the financial center of the country, and also the center for car manufacturing.

In comparison with the other regions, the coastal desert is highly industrialized and has the most intensive agricultural systems. The irrigated desert is very fertile, and in the north, sugarcane, rice, and cotton are cultivated. South of Lima the conditions are ideal for grapes, fruit, and olives. Throughout the desert there are many chicken farms, which produced 66 million chickens in 1992.

Fishing is a very important part of the Peruvian economy, with fish meal and canning industries earning valuable income from export.

Traditionally, the northern part of the coast has been the center of Peru's oil industry, with major onshore and offshore oilfields near Talara.

A fish meal-processing plant at Chimbote. Peru earned $427 million in fish meal exports in 1995. Fish meal, which consists of ground-up fish, has many uses. It is especially used as a fertilizer on crops and as animal feed.

THE COAST FACT BOX	
Proportion of Peru covered:	11 % (54,584 sq. mi.)
Proportion of Peru's population:	52.2 % (11,818,080)
Economy:	Fishing and fish-meal industries. Manufacturing industries of textiles, food processing, and automobiles. Intensive agriculture.
Climate:	Temperate with an average annual temperature of 65°F.
Average rainfall:	Most areas less than 1 inch.

Right Small fishing boats in Chimbote harbor. In the 1980s, overfishing led to the collapse of the fishing industry, although it has now recovered.

SOCIAL CONDITIONS

The population of the coastal region has the best access to health care, education, and employment in Peru. For this reason many people leave the Andes and migrate to cities like Lima, Trujillo, and Chimbote. The coast has a higher proportion of professional people, such as engineers, teachers, and civil servants, than the other regions. However, the living conditions of the coastal poor are often appalling. For example, more than half of Lima's 6.3 million population live in shantytowns. Most of these people have no running water and have to buy untreated water by the barrel.

The working conditions in the fishing industry and in agriculture are often very unhealthy with frequent accidents and exposure to toxic chemicals.

Left Industrial pollution is a threat to the health of many Peruvians. This steel foundry causes serious air pollution.

Villa El Salvador

Villa El Salvador is a shantytown built in the desert dunes about 12 miles south of Lima. It is more than just a squatter settlement, because it is an example of what is possible when people work together. It was founded in May 1971 by a wave of 10,000 migrants, escaping the devastation of an earthquake near Huaraz in the Andes. At first the police tried to expel the squatters, killing one of the community leaders, Edilberto Ramos, but eventually they were permitted to stay. By keeping the Andean tradition of community organization, they were able to improve the area.

Today, 300,000 people live in mud brick or concrete houses, and most have running water and electricity. All these improvements were done without government help. The community has also transformed the desert into farming land for cotton, fruit, and dairy cattle by watering the area with treated sewage.

"We are the only district of Lima that does not throw its sewage into the sea...we are now trying to collect sewage from other districts to irrigate the rest of the desert."
—Michel Azcueta, former mayor of Villa El Salvador

A street child drinking from the fountain outside the presidential palace in Lima

SLUMS OF HOPE

Fifty years ago the majority of Peruvians lived in the countryside, but now more than 70 percent of the population live in towns and cities. This growth in the urban population has led to a rise in the number of shantytowns or slums. These settlements are usually situated around cities, often on steeply sloping land or on areas generally unsuitable for conventional housing.

Migrants arriving in Lima come from areas where there is severe poverty and high unemployment. But these people tend to be relatively young and better educated than the national average. Migrants do not usually make their way to slums immediately but live first in poor-quality, rented accommodations. After a while they may make the decision to move to a slum, often as part of a group of people who have carefully planned the occupation of an empty piece of land. Residents quickly put up shelters made of matting or whatever else is handy. As money becomes available, they gradually improve the buildings. The slums usually develop without such basic services as water, sewerage, and electricity. Once they become firmly established, the government will, at last, provide basic services such as sanitation. Throughout this process, the communities within the slums work together to improve the conditions in which they live.

Living conditions in slums like this one in Lima are often harsh, especially compared with the comfortable conditions that richer Peruvians can afford.

FISHING

The fishing and fish meal industries have traditionally been high earners of foreign income. During the 1960s and 1970s, Peru's fish catches increased. In 1971, Peru caught more than 10 million tons of *anchoveta* (Peruvian anchovy) alone and produced 2 million tons of fish meal. But Peru was taking more than the fish stocks could support. This, along with the arrival of the warm sea current *El Niño* in 1973, which caused many schools of fish to migrate away from Peru, reduced the catch to just 1.5 million tons.

The fish stocks have been recovering ever since, and in 1992, the total catch was 8.4 million tons, then more than 10 million tons in 1993. In 1995, Peru produced 2,348 tons of fish meal, which accounted for 52 per cent of world production, earning $427 million in exports.

Many experts believe that the quantity of fish now being caught is once again more than the marine environment can support, and they are predicting another crash in fish numbers. The situation will be made worse by the coastal pollution caused by the fish-processing and other industries.

"Every 2.5 acres of shrimp lagoon produces a harvest worth about $10,000, and it is possible to get 2–2.5 harvests a year. The 6,000 acres of shrimp lagoons in operation now form an important part of the economy."
—a shrimp farm manager, near Tumbes

EL NIÑO

The Peruvian coast is kept cool by the cold Humboldt current, which flows north toward the equator. But every five or six years a warm current, known as El Niño (which translates as "the child"), is blown south, causing the temperature of the coastal waters to rise. This in turn causes schools of fish to migrate.

When El Niño comes, the evaporation from the warm sea is so great that the coast receives torrential rain. In 1983, areas of the north coast that normally receive little annual rain experienced more than six feet of rainfall in the months of January and February, causing widespread damage.

This man sells fish caught close to the mangrove coast, near Puerto Pizarro in northern Peru.

Mangroves and Shrimp Farming

"*In 1982 there were 14,000 acres of mangroves near Tumbes, but 3,000 acres have been destroyed to make shrimp farms. Along with other factors, the area of mangroves has been reduced to only 11,200 acres.*"
—**Manuel Leiva, Peruvian Foundation for the Conservation of Nature**

Peru has a small area of mangrove trees along the most northern part of the Pacific coast. Mangroves are extremely important because they regulate the quality of seawater, and help prevent coastal erosion. They are also the breeding grounds for countless marine organisms, many of which have commercial value.

Peru's shrimp farming industry is located in the mangrove forests. Shrimp farming is a profitable business, which is helped by the excellent water quality created by the trees. It is an important part of the north coast economy, employing thousands of people.

Shrimp larvae are caught by *laveros* working with fine mesh nets up and down the coast. These are then released into lagoons of 7 to 10 acres, made in the mangrove forest.

Above
Manuel Leiva with mangrove seed pods
Right
Farmed shrimps from a mangrove lagoon

The larvae grow rapidly and are then harvested and sold.

Unfortunately, there are many environmental problems associated with shrimp farming. Each time a shrimp lagoon is dug, an area of mangroves is destroyed. A cocktail of feed, waste, and chemicals used to help the shrimp's growth removes the oxygen from the mangroves around the lagoon and seriously affects fish life.

Cotton plantations like this one have been important to the economy of the coastal region for many years. Recently, however, the world price of cotton has fallen. This has reduced the amount Peru can earn by exporting cotton.

COTTON

Cotton is native to Peru and was first cultivated more than 4,000 years ago. Cotton cloth was used to wrap the mummified bodies of the dead of many desert cultures, and perhaps the finest weavings ever made were buried with the Paracas mummies of about 400 B.C.

Cotton growing is ideally suited to irrigated desert conditions. In Piura it is possible to grow the valuable Pima cotton, which has extra long fibers. Peru also produces naturally colored cotton. The cotton husks are used as cattle feed.

However, over the past decade, the importance of cotton in Peru has been declining due to lack of investment and a large increase in cotton prices. In 1989, cotton production was 321,000 tons, falling to 97,800 tons in 1993. Production is now recovering, but because of the addition of chemicals and constant irrigation, soils are becoming exhausted.

MAIN COTTON PRODUCTION AREAS	
Ica	43 %
Lima	15 %
Piura	31 %

The Andean Region

MIGRATION AND RURAL COMMUNITIES

The Andean region is a high land of gentle slopes surrounded by groups of towering mountains and has an average altitude of more than 9,800 feet. Although there are plateaus suitable for cultivation, the population has become too large for such a poor agricultural area.

Most people in the countryside live in scattered villages or lone households. Although Spanish is the official language of Peru, many people speak only Quechua or Aymara (used around Lake Titicaca in the south). Over the last 30 years, many people have left the Andean region for the cities of the coastal and Amazon regions. They were encouraged by the government, which wanted to reduce rural poverty in the Andes.

— Major roads
••••• Railroads
⚓ Major ports
✈ Major airports

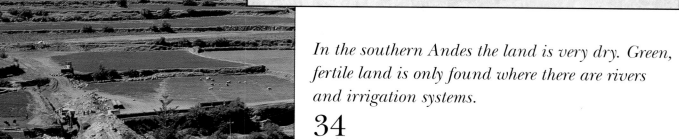

THE ANDEAN FACT BOX

Proportion of Peru covered: 27 % (134,000 sq. mi.)

Proportion of Peru's population: 35.7 % (8,082,480)

Economy: Mining, subsistence agriculture, and tourism.

Climate: Cool, with average annual temperatures in the populated areas of 52°F to 61°F.

Average rainfall: Up to 39 inches on northern and eastern slopes.

In the southern Andes the land is very dry. Green, fertile land is only found where there are rivers and irrigation systems.

34

La Oroya

La Oroya is one of the worst examples of the Peruvian mining industry. In 1922, an American company called Cerro de Pasco built a smelter at La Oroya. It was designed to process lead and copper and provided employment for 3,000 to 5,000 Andean people. However, because of a combination of bad design and poor location, the smelter poisoned 1,700,000 acres of land. The fumes from the smelter had very high levels of lead and arsenic, and a survey in 1952 found the levels of lead in the atmosphere at La Oroya to be 125 times higher than international safety limits. The pollution devastated the rural economy of a particularly good agricultural area, and most land-owners were forced into selling their land to the mining company. After 1965, the smelter improved its emissions, but there are still high levels of lead and arsenic in the atmosphere.

This smelter at La Oroya has so far polluted 1,700,000 acres of land, causing serious health problems in the local population.

MINING AND SMALL-SCALE AGRICULTURE

Mining has been an important part of the Andean economy since the conquest by the Spanish. The industry has been a key sector of the economy for hundreds of years and typically accounts for about half the value of Peru's exports, although in 1993 it fell to 41.3 percent (earning $1.432 billion).

The mining population is made up almost entirely of Andean Indian laborers, numbering about 80,000 until the end of the 1980s. The working conditions are tough: some mines are as high in the Andes as 17,000 feet. During the 1990s, there have been a number of problems for the industry. The main problem is that Peru's minerals no longer fetch such a high price on the world's markets.

*"In the morning, it is not possible to see from one side of the valley to the other because of the pollution, and it makes it difficult to breathe... For a contract worker the wage is 15 soles [about $6] a day, while a regular worker earns about 20 soles [about $8] a day." —**Juan Chavez***

The Uros Floating Islands and Tourism

The floating Uros islands on Lake Titicaca are made from reeds. The reeds are replaced regularly because the water rots them away.

Dotted across the surface of Lake Titicaca are the Uros floating islands, which are constructed from local reeds. The islands are named after the Uro Indians who used to inhabit them, but the last full-blooded Uro Indian died in 1959. Severe poverty drove many Uro Indians from the islands; they intermarried with the Aymara and Quechua-speaking Indians in and around Puno. Now some of the Indians have returned to the island to follow the Uro way of life.

Tourism is a major part of Uros island life now. Regular tour groups visit the islands, and the islanders have altered their way of life and their handicrafts to suit the tourists. In this way they have lost part of their culture. But the conditions on the islands are so poor that without tourism the Indians could not stay there at all.

Copper is Peru's single most important export, earning $658 million in 1993 and $806 million in 1992. Peru is also one of the world's top three silver producers (worth $76 million in 1993), while the possibility of exceeding 40 tons of gold a year is helping to encourage foreign investment in the Peruvian mining industry.

In 1993, Peru produced 665,000 tons of zinc worth $258 million and 218,000 tons of lead worth $131 million.

In contrast to the coastal industries, the agriculture of the Andean region, or sierra, is mainly carried out on a subsistence basis. Farmers with small plots of land produce enough food for their families to eat or to trade locally. The main crops are corn, potatoes, barley (for the beer industry), and beans. Much of the land is hard to grow crops on, so sheep, alpacas, and llamas are herded on the higher slopes, providing wool and meat.

An Andean farmer uses a wooden plow pulled by oxen.

TOURISM

Tourism is a new industry in the Andes. About half a million tourists visited Peru in 1995, and many of the country's main attractions are in the Andean region, especially around the old Inca capital city of Cuzco.

"Now that the tourists are returning to Peru it means that there will be more work in Cuzco… It means that the young people will not have go to Lima to find work."
—Modesto Chalco

LOWEST LIVING STANDARDS IN PERU

The living conditions of the Andean region are not only poor by Peruvian standards, but also among the worst anywhere in South America. The infant mortality rate rises to more than twice the national average in some areas, and malnutrition is commonplace. Malnutrition makes children more susceptible to respiratory illnesses such as tuberculosis.

The Andean region has poor roads, schools, and hospitals in comparison with the coast. Because most of the Andean population lives in rural locations, providing basic services is difficult.

The Amazon Region

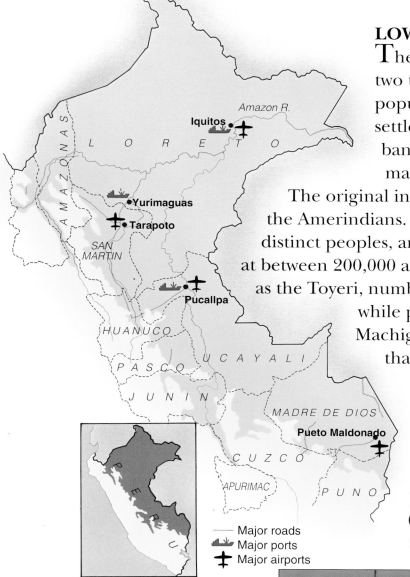

Major roads
Major ports
Major airports

LOW POPULATION DENSITY

The Amazon region covers nearly two thirds of Peru but has a very low population density. Today, most settlements are crowded on to river banks, because the rivers serve as the main forest highways.

The original inhabitants of Peru's rain forest are the Amerindians. There are approximately 60 distinct peoples, and estimates put their population at between 200,000 and 250,000. Some peoples, such as the Toyeri, number only a handful of individuals, while peoples such as the Ashaninka and Machiguenga have populations of more than 10,000.

The Amazon region has become home to an increasing number of nonindigenous settlers. In towns like Iquitos, thousands of migrants arrived from different places during the rubber boom (between 1890 and 1910), and many of these settled. In recent

A ferry boat near Pucallpa. People use these boats to travel through the waterways of the Amazon River. There are few roads in the Amazon region, which makes land travel difficult. Because of its low population density, the building of roads in this area is not seen as an important benefit to the Peruvian people.

decades, thousands of poor migrants have again flooded into the Amazonian region in search of agricultural land and gold.

TIMBER, OIL, AND GOLD

Because the rain forest ecosystem is very delicate, a relatively small proportion of the land, less than 10 percent, is suitable for agriculture. In 1993, only 1,100,000 acres were under cultivation. Where conditions are favorable, rubber, jute (fiber from tree bark used to make mats and sacking), rice, and coffee are grown. However, cattle ranching and the timber industry are also important. Because of the lack of good transportation links with the coast and, in particular, with the port of Callao, the region has developed slowly. At present the only route for transporting heavy goods from Iquitos to Callao, which are 626 miles apart, involves a 6,990-mile journey by ship via the Panama Canal. In the last 20 years, discoveries of huge oil, gas, and gold reserves in the Amazon region have added to the region's economic potential.

THE AMAZON FACT BOX	
Proportion of Peru covered:	62 % (307,659 mi²)
Proportion of Peru's population:	12.1 % (2,739,440)
Economy:	Agriculture and untapped mineral wealth.
Climate:	Very hot with average annual temperature of 88°F.
Average rainfall:	39 inches in lowlands and up to 117 inches on eastern slopes of the Andes.

Above *A man employed by a sawmill in Pucallpa checks that the logs are firmly attached to a strong rope, before they are pulled out of the river to be sawed into planks.*

Left *Part of an oil well in the Amazon rain forest in Peru*

Manu National Park

Manu is the largest rain forest park in the world, covering an area of 3.7 million acres (roughly half the size of Switzerland). It is an area of extraordinary biological richness and includes many types of habitats between altitudes of 656 feet and 13,780 feet.

In one 2 sq. mi. area, researchers have found approximately 10 percent of the world's species of bird and over 1,000 plant species. There are populations of 17 endangered animals and birds within the reserve, including the spectacled bear, the puma, and cock of the rock in the Andean area, and jaguar, harpy eagle, giant river otter, and woolly monkey in the Amazon area.

The park is now providing a refuge from the pressures of logging, cattle raising, and colonists. This refuge is not only for the wildlife but also for a number of Amerindian peoples, including groups of Machiguenga and the uncontacted Kugapakori.

With regards to oil, Peru is virtually self-sufficient. In 1993, it produced 46,096 barrels and exported $181 million of heavy crude oil in the same year. In the Amazon alone there are 200 million acres of oil-bearing structures. Shell is currently conducting a feasibility study of the Camisea gas field, which is estimated to have 366 billion cubic yards of gas (equivalent to 2 million barrels of oil).

A woolly monkey hangs by its tail from a large Amazonian tree in Manu National Park.

Top A small Amazonian fish market, where a wide variety of fish are sold

Bottom Many houses in the Amazon region are on stilts because the rivers rise and fall with the wet and dry seasons.

THE AMERINDIAN POPULATION

The Amerindian population has suffered terribly over the last 500 years. When the first Europeans invaded Amerindian lands, they greatly reduced the Amerindian population, both by the western diseases they brought to Peru and by outright murder. The government still does not recognize boundaries to many traditional lands, and missionary activity, tourists, and racial prejudice continue to undermine traditional beliefs.

The discovery of gold deposits in some of the main rivers led to mercury contamination (the miners used mercury to sift the gold), further affecting the lives of all the forest's inhabitants. Malnutrition is not as serious a problem as in the Andean region because of the abundant fruit and fish.

Recently, violence has become a widespread problem in the northern rain forest because of the illegal cultivation of coca for the manufacture of cocaine.

The Shipibo Cooperative

The Shipibo people live near the town of Pucallpa. They have a long history of contact with the non-indigenous settlers in the area.

A Shipibo Amerindian family in their house on the shores of Lake Yarinococho

Unlike many contacted groups the Shipibo people have retained much of their traditional way of life. On the shores of Lake Yarinacocha, about two hours by boat from Pucallpa, the Shipibo operate a co-operative where they produce pottery, textiles, and other artifacts of traditional design that they sell to tourists and collectors.

"Many tourists now visit us to buy our pots and cloths, which helps our community...our eldest son is now studying at University in Pucallpa."
—Lebanita Rodriguez Renhijo

THE COCA LEAF

Coca is Peru's most important agricultural export, earning an estimated $1 billion annually. However, the cultivation and trade in coca is illegal. Almost all is grown to be processed into cocaine and smuggled into the United States and Europe.

The coca leaf has been part of Peruvian life for thousands of years; coca leaves have been found in Peruvian graves dating back to 2000 B.C. In the Andes today, they still have an important religious and ceremonial use as an offering to the spirit world, and coca leaves are burned to drive away evil.

The coca plant grows well between altitudes of 3,000 feet and 8,000 feet. Its leaves contain small quantities of 14 different alkaloids, released when the leaves are chewed with lime. These lessen the appetite, deaden pain, and increase stamina. Andean women chew coca leaves during

labor to ease childbirth, while the men commonly chew coca to help make strenuous work more bearable. Around the world, modern surgeons use cocaine as a local anaesthetic in ear, nose, and throat surgery.

However, cocaine is often misused. It is an extremely dangerous drug that can kill; therefore, it is illegal to own and sell it (unless used for medical purposes). Yet through illegal trade, Peru's cocaine industry continues to develop, encouraged through rising demand and by higher prices. By 1993, 741,000 acres were under coca cultivation, with 300,000 people involved full-time or part-time in its growth. Peru produces 60 percent of the world's coca, but the combination of illegality and enormous profits has brought violence to much of the northern Amazon region.

Above These are the leaves of a coca plant. Coca grows on the low foothills where the Andes and the Amazon meet.

Left Coca leaves being picked near the town of Quillabamba. Although it is used to produce an illegal drug, coca is a valuable export to Peru's economy.

The Future

Peru is a country with great potential. It has enormous untapped natural resources and mineral wealth. The challenge that faces Peru today is how best to exploit this natural wealth for the good of the whole nation, without ruining the environment. This means breaking the pattern of development, where Lima and the coastal cities have historically enjoyed the majority of the economic benefits. It also means planning for the long term, because in the past Peru has been subject to what is known as a "boom or bust" economy. This is where resources, such as Pacific fish stocks, have been exploited with little regard for the future. This gives a short-lived rise ("boom") to the economy followed by a dramatic collapse of fish stocks, and, hence, the national economy ("bust"). Environmental and social problems also need to be cut down because, as can be seen in the example of the lead and copper smelter at La Oroya on page 35, economic benefits for one part of the economy, such as the mining industry, were equaled by the devastation experienced in other sectors, such as agriculture.

Over the last 50 years, Peru has seen significant economic development, but this has largely been restricted to the coastal region. The difficult terrain of Peru presents great problems for progress and communications. The Incas and the other great Pre-Columbian civilizations have shown, however, that the difficult terrain should not block Peru's development. In fact, the Incas were not only able to group together large areas by organized communication, but they were also able

A view of the Rimac River, which is the main river in Lima, and the accumulated trash on its banks

to spread economic and social benefits more evenly than in modern Peru.

In the 1990s, Peru has begun to change, and the conditions of the general population have started to improve gradually. Under President Fujimori, terrorism that once affected the lives of millions of Peruvians and devastated the economy has been greatly reduced. The once-bankrupt economy has been converted into the fastest-growing economy of South America, and tourists and foreign investors are returning.

Peru has also found itself well positioned to take advantage of the rapidly growing economies of the Asian countries, on the other side of the Pacific Ocean.

History has shown that Peruvians are resourceful people, and all their ingenuity will be required to tackle the appalling conditions that millions of people now have to suffer. This will mean looking for new and appropriate solutions to Peru's problems.

A young girl using a computer in a school in Lima. President Fujimori has made education a top priority for Peru.

Glossary

Alkaloids Basic groups of chemicals found in certain plants.

APRA A socialist political party in Peru.

Colonization One country's attempt to govern and sometimes occupy another country.

Constitution A written record of the principles and rules by which a country or state is governed.

Effluent Sewage or industrial waste flowing into a river or sea.

Fertilizer Materials that enhance plant growth.

Gross Domestic Product (GDP) The total wealth a country produces in a year.

Guerrilla organization An independent fighting movement, fighting for its own causes and often fighting against the official military of its country.

Guano Accumulation of bird droppings rich in nitrates and phosphates.

Human rights The basic rights laid down by international law to which all people should be entitled.

Indigenous The original inhabitants of a particular region.

Inflation A general increase in prices.

Infrastructure The basic foundations of a country, such as roads, bridges, and sewers.

Investment Money that is put into a business activity in order to profit from it.

Irrigation A system of man-made channels through which water is encouraged to flow. This supplies dry land with water, so that plants can be grown.

Laveros The fishermen who specialize in catching shrimp larvae for shrimp farms.

Malnutrition A condition caused by a lack of foods and essential nutrients necessary for growth.

Mangroves Tropical trees that grow only in seawater and have distinctive, twisting roots growing above the water.

Mestizos People of mixed Indian and European race.

Migration The movement from one place to live in another.

Nitrate A chemical compound that increases plant growth.

Oases Fertile spots in deserts where water is found.

Per capita income The country's GDP divided by the number of people in that country.

Plateaus High, flat pieces of land.

Smelter A place where metals are extracted from their ores.

Subsidized Money contributed by a government or state to make a product or service cheaper to use or buy.

Subsistence The system of producing or earning sufficient money or food to survive, without making a profit.

Temperate A climate characterized by mild temperatures.

Further Information

Friends of the Earth (U.S.A.), 218 D Street SE, Washington, DC 20003 can provide information on environmental issues.

OXFAM America, 115 Broadway, Boston, MA 02116, has a special education program and produces publications, videotapes, slides, and leaflets.

UNICEF, 1 UN Plaza, New York, NY 10017, can provide information on the plight of the world's children.

Books to Read

Blue, Rose and Corinne Naden. *Andes Mountains* (Wonders of the World Series). Austin, TX: Raintree Steck-Vaughn, 1994.

Lepthein, Emile U. *Peru* (Enchantment of the World Series). Chicago: Childrens Press, 1992.

Lerner Publications, Department of Geography Staff. *Peru in Pictures* (Visual Geography Series). Minneapolis: Lerner Publications, 1994.

Morrison, Marion. *Ecuador, Peru, and Bolivia.* Austin, TX: Raintree Steck-Vaughn, 1992.

Index

Numbers in **bold** refer to illustrations as well as text.